Go Superlambananas
The Book

Woodland Publishing

ISBN 978-1-905547-10-4

Woodland Publishing
Publisher: Guy Woodland
Editor-in-Chief: Lew Baxter
'Go Superlambananas: The Book', Editor: Fiona Shaw

This book stems from an original idea by Fiona Shaw. It is published by Guy Woodland in a collaboration with Fiona Shaw and Wild in Art and with the endorsement of Taro Chiezo, the 'SuperLambBanana' creator.

Editing and writing: Fiona Shaw, Lew Baxter
German translating: Alexandra Wolkowicz
Photography: Ed Ball, Pete Carr, Fiona Shaw, Guy Woodland, Tate Liverpool
Proof reading: Judy Tasker
Printed and bound: China
First published in 2008 by Guy Woodland in association with Cities500 as a 21st Century Cities publication
Reprinted in October 2009 by Guy Woodland

Studio and Office:
No 2 The Old Stables, Charles Road, Wirral, UK
Tel: + 44 (0) 151 632 3280
Skype: +44 (0) 151 324 1273
e.mail: info@cities500.com
www.cities500.com
© Guy Woodland - November 2008

SuperLambBanana turns pink

Contents

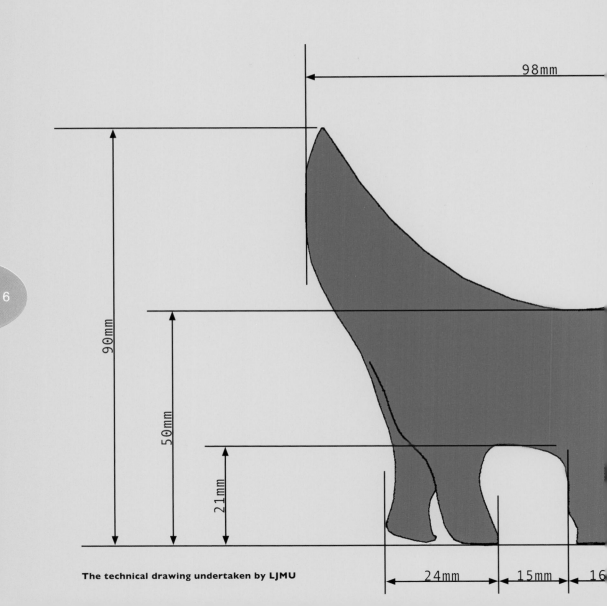

98mm

90mm

50mm

21mm

6

The technical drawing undertaken by LJMU

24mm

15mm

16

Partners and Friends

Liverpool Culture Company
Northwest Regional Development Agency
Liverpool John Moores University
Wild in Art
Finch – the ideas agency

Liverpool Vision
FACT
Tate Liverpool
Utility
TJ Morris Ltd
Chime Creative Management
The Riverside Group

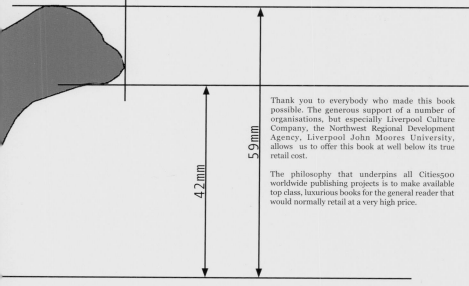

Thank you to everybody who made this book possible. The generous support of a number of organisations, but especially Liverpool Culture Company, the Northwest Regional Development Agency, Liverpool John Moores University, allows us to offer this book at well below its true retail cost.

The philosophy that underpins all Cities500 worldwide publishing projects is to make available top class, luxurious books for the general reader that would normally retail at a very high price.

SuperLambBanana on the Dock Road

Acknowledgements
Lew Baxter and Guy Woodland

Cities500 Publishing

There were ripples of excitement mingled with scepticism when, in the summer of 2008, a herd of 'baby' superlambananas started appearing all over Liverpool and even beyond the city boundaries, some even dismissively commenting that these 'mini-clones' of sculptor Taro Chiezo's original were merely trivialising art. The critics were proved so wrong.

These enchanting creatures captured the hearts and minds of Liverpudlians, tourists and, indeed, everyone who came in contact with them. The 'offspring' of SuperLambBanana became magnets for children and adults alike, with crowds buzzing around them.

It was, in fact, a magical 'happening' called *Go Superlambananas* dreamed up by the Wild in Art team working with the Liverpool Culture Company as part of the city's European Capital of Culture year. It turned into a cult that no one could have anticipated. There are even those who believe that superlambananas ousted the Liver Birds as the emblem of Liverpool.

The jury is still out on that but when Fiona Shaw, a Liverpool-based writer, approached us with the idea of publishing a photographic commemoration of this joyful event, we were fired up. It got the immediate endorsement of Wild in Art's Sally-Ann Wilkinson, to whom we owe our grateful thanks. We set about photographing all of the creatures in their various locations before they were brought in for the grand auction that raised thousands of pounds for the Lord Mayor of Liverpool's charity appeal. There was certainly passion during the bidding, not least by Tom and Joe Morris from TJ Morris Ltd (Home Bargains) who personally bought 17 of the creatures.

We passed the book idea by Phil Redmond (see his foreword) aboard the sailing ship *Zebu* when he helped launch our *Liverpool: World Waterfront City* book. He loved it, as did Kris Donaldson, chief executive of the Liverpool Culture Company, and Peter Mearns, marketing and communications director of the Northwest Regional Development Agency. Further support was quickly – and enthusiastically - given by Michael Brown, vice chancellor of Liverpool John Moores University. And there are a many others who deserve our gratitude.

We hope this book will be our thanks to them, and a lasting legacy to both Taro Chiezo's astonishing creation and the fabulous *Go Superlambananas* event that captivated Liverpool and the world.

December 2008

J. NICKELS & SONS LTD. SAILMAKERS

R & SONS | SHIPS CHANDLE

SuperLambBanana turns into a cow overnight
as part of a student prank

SuperLambBanana: the original

Taro Chiezo's iconic SuperLambBanana (SLB) made its first spectacular and somewhat controversial appearance on the streets of Liverpool in 1998 as part of the ArtTranspennine98 exhibition. Chiezo had first created a model of the hybrid beast just four inches tall and that was brought to towering 17-foot life by local sculptor Andy Small, Julian Taylor, Tommy Reason and Ray Stokes.

ArtTranspennine created a trail of 30 art installations between Liverpool and Hull and SuperLambBanana – in a partnership with Tate Liverpool and the Henry Moore Foundation – was unveiled at that year's Tate reopening.

Chiezo's SuperLambBanana was intended as a fusion of thoughts about the future and the past at a time when Liverpool was leaving behind a rather troubled recent history to become a centre of excellence for medical science and hi-tech engineering.

Originally exhibited at a New York gallery, it took an ironic swipe at genetic engineering and, later, Liverpool-specific interpretations saw in it a representation of the city's traditional role as a port, exporting Lancashire wool and importing Fyffes bananas.

Small and his team, based at the Bryant & May matchworks in Garston, created the beast on a 1:50 scale using eight tonnes of concrete, steel and wire mesh and a foam-filled steel base. The sculpture is hollow concrete built around a mesh structure, making it relatively light and transportable, yet hardwearing and resilient.

Lewis Biggs, now director of the Liverpool Biennial, was director of Tate Liverpool at the time. He says: 'I'd seen Taro's work in Tokyo and he looked to be a very good sculptor. So I commissioned him to create something new – but we didn't know what he would come up with. The rest is history. It's popular because of its quirkiness. People can interpret it any way they like, that is the beauty of art.'

It was like nothing Liverpool had ever seen before and initial reaction was often confused. Its bright yellow glow attracted attention – often for the wrong reasons – but, after a renegade attack saw the SuperLambBanana painted with Friesian spots, Liverpool saw the funny side and took the giant sculpture to its heart. The penny had dropped.

At the end of ArtTranspennine the SLB was handed over to the Liverpool Architecture & Design Trust for safekeeping and was moved from its resting place adjacent to the tunnel ventilation tower on Mann Island, first to Williamson Square, then Spike Island, Wapping and – its current home – outside the Liverpool John Moores University Avril Robarts Centre on Tithebarn Street.

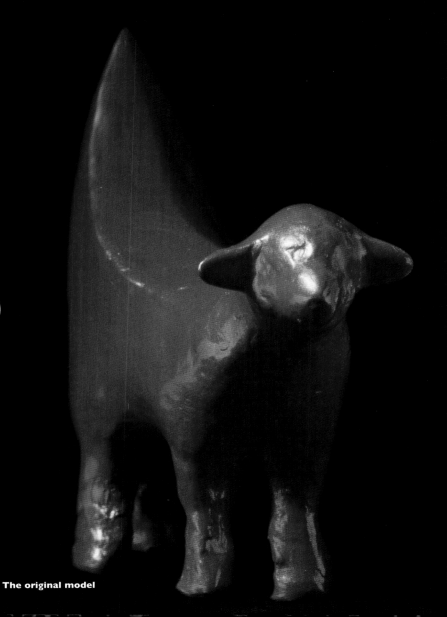

12

The original model

The Birth of SuperLambBanana
Janet Martin

Director of Corporate Communications
Liverpool John Moores University

When Japanese-based artist Taro Chiezo created his strangely compelling figure in 1998 as part of the ArtTranspennine Exhibition he could have no idea that 10 years later his unusual artwork would come to symbolise the playful nature of a city celebrating its year as Capital of Culture.

And LJMU has been part of the story from the very beginning.

The SuperLambBanana was originally created to warn of the dangers of genetically modified food. The small prototype model created by Chiezo was chosen for part of the exhibition at the Tate Liverpool and LJMU artists were commissioned to create the large sculpture that is seen around the city today.

Dr Richard Gant, Head of Fine Art at LJMU, remembers the challenge: 'The Tate wanted to display the SuperLambBanana as a large form installation. The original piece was very small and in order to scale the model for the exhibition we had to work on the ergonomics of the design, particularly the tail.'

Getting the balance of the model right was crucial and Richard worked with Ian Wroot of the LJMU architecture department on the sculpture that was exhibited in the Tate in 1998. That piece was only one-third of the size of the city's iconic sculpture that now sits outside the university's faculty of health.

Standing 17 foot tall, the Superlambbanana was made in the Matchbox Factory by LJMU fine art students under Richard Gant's supervision.

It may have been planted in Liverpool to signify the city's history as a port trading in lambs and the import of bananas, but in the year of Capital of Culture, and with over 100 customised replicas on the streets, the SuperLambBanana has become as symbolic of Liverpool as the famous Liver Birds.

Foreword
Taro Chiezo

Artist

'I am very glad the people of Liverpool love my sculpture so much. I remember when I began working on SuperLambBanana. First, I started researching the city's history and even old ghost stories. I talked with many people in Liverpool and, finally, the work took shape. SuperLambBanana became one of the major works of my career.

After the first exhibition an art dealer wanted me to sell it to a museum in Japan, but instead I talked with the director of the Tate gallery and we decided to loan SuperLambBanana to Liverpool.

I am glad that Liverpool will continue to be SuperLambBanana's permanent home.'

December 2008

Foreword
Professor Phil Redmond CBE

Chairman, National Museums Liverpool
and Chairman, Merseyfilm

It is often easy to forget that every human endeavour starts with an idea. Sometimes, more than often, the idea comes from one person but is put into practice by others. So it has been with 2008.

One idea, to make Liverpool the European Capital of Culture, has been defined, delivered and put into practice by many people. If one project epitomised that process it was *Go Superlambananas*. More importantly, it also came to symbolise how ideas need to resonate with the zeitgeist.

Originally commissioned in 1998, perhaps as an artist's individual challenge for humanity to consider the dangers of genetically modified food, SuperLambBanana was initially met with bafflement verging on ignorant derision. Yet, a decade later, it has come to signify the power of allowing people to participate in and create culture, rather than simply consume it; this in itself is one of the principal themes of 2008.

Building on the original idea, the next stage was to take the basic form, a blank white replica, and throw out a challenge to both artists and community groups to use it as a canvas on which to present their own interpretation or challenge to and of the world. The results, as you will see in this book, are truly fascinating; from the individual designs to the naming of the individual concepts.

They represent a range of talent, opinion, humour, skill and expression that reflects the people of Liverpool, the zeitgeist of 2008 and the city's term as European Capital of Culture. That is why two have been acquired to sit in the permanent collections of National Museums Liverpool. So that future generations may look back on them and be reminded that everything starts with an idea.

I hope you enjoy this publication, as much as the people of Liverpool enjoyed *Go Superlambananas*.

Foreword
Professor Michael Brown CBE, DL

Chief Executive and Vice Chancellor
Liverpool John Moores University

This book celebrates the affectionate relationship between the people of Liverpool and the SuperLambBanana. In a highly individual city where humour and idiosyncrasy are cherished, this unique sculpture has quickly been adopted as an emblem of the city.

My acquaintance with the SuperLambBanana began when I first arrived in Liverpool in 2000 as Vice Chancellor and Chief Executive of Liverpool John Moores University. Only eight years ago the city looked very different from the Liverpool of today. There were endless examples of beautiful historic buildings, but much of the new architecture was only just emerging, so that the university struggled to select images for its prospectus that symbolised the modern Liverpool. We chose the SuperLambBanana, which effortlessly represents a city that embraces innovative art and ideas.

In 2004, having contributed in some small way to securing the UNESCO World Heritage Site accolade, I was asked to contribute to a book that celebrated this achievement for the city, and to have my picture taken alongside one of the best-known Liverpool landmarks – but didn't have any choice as to which one. I was delighted when it turned out to be the SuperLambBanana, and that very photograph appears in this book.

The SuperLambBanana is a dramatic work of art with immediate visual impact. During redevelopment work it had to be moved from its former site on the Strand, and I suggested to the City Council that LJMU would be delighted to 'host' the sculpture outside our Learning Resource Centre on Tithebarn Street, where it now stands proudly guarding the entrance. I had not however realised until very recently that LJMU's own School of Art had had a significant role in its construction, as outlined elsewhere.

In early 2009, LJMU's new £28m Art and Design Academy will open, offering gallery space and a café for the public, housed in one of Liverpool's leading-edge signature buildings designed by Rick Mather. As a long-time fan, I can imagine how relocation within the public Sculpture Park beside this facility would allow the SuperLambBanana to be viewed and enjoyed in a tranquil setting alongside other works of art.

INTRODUCTION
Sally-Ann Wilkinson and Charles Langhorne

Directors, Wild in Art

One day last June something very funny happened. Almost overnight, quietly and without fuss, 125 incredible creatures invaded the streets and public spaces of the region. Some were painted, others adorned with intricate mosaic, while more were covered in photographs. All of them were individual works of art. Their arrival may have been almost unnoticed, but their impact on the city and its people could not have been greater. The superlambananas had arrived.

For 10 weeks during the summer of 2008, thousands of people embraced public art and took huge enjoyment from exploring the city and discovering 125 superlambananas, beautifully created by the artists and residents of Liverpool.

The ambition that underpinned our plan for *Go Superlambananas* was to create a mass participation public art event, bringing together the business and creative sectors with local communities to celebrate the spirit of fun and rich diversity at the heart of Liverpool. It was to be an event created by Liverpool people for the enjoyment of both residents and visitors alike.

As Wild in Art, the company commissioned to produce the event, we wanted the trail of art sculptures to weave into the very heart of those communities that created the superlambananas. And we wanted people to be 'visitors in their own city', so we deliberately planned the trail so that it would include familiar and iconic places as well as go to recently regenerated areas such as the waterfront, before heading west across to the Wirral and south to Runcorn – there was even a superlambanana at the top of Moel Famau and one at London's Euston station.

The iconic SuperLambBanana sculpture, originally the vision of Japanese artist Taro Chiezo in 1998, provided the perfect inspiration to create a street-size 3D canvas to celebrate Liverpool – its people, its places, its heritage, regeneration and world-renowned arts scene.

The event was 12 months in the planning. We set up an office with a core team of four professionals specialising in artist liaison, sponsorship, marketing and public relations and logistics and embarked on the ambitious task of persuading companies, community groups, artists and individuals to get involved.

We feel immensely proud and appreciative that we encountered so many people who embraced the vision and, through their generosity and 'can do' attitude, enabled this ambitious, citywide event to take place.

Through sponsorship support, we were able to commission over 100 Liverpool-based professional and talented artists to produce their designs, as well as many individual art projects involving 26 local community groups. Artists worked day and night in the painting space at the Matchworks, creating an outstanding showcase incorporating many different art media – from graffiti to fine art, mosaic and textile.

The lengthy roll call of supporters made this the largest multi-sponsorship art project ever to take place in the United Kingdom. With local media support, including the Daily Post and Liverpool Echo and region-wide competitions run by both BBC North West Tonight and ITV Granada Reports, as well as individual sponsors, *Go Superlambananas* proved to be the perfect platform for people to bring artistic endeavour into their homes, workplaces and schools, furthering the debate about the importance of creativity in our everyday lives.

But what has made *Go Superlambananas* so special is the generosity of spirit, warmth and enthusiasm of not only the people who participated directly in the event, but the thousands more who have taken great pleasure visiting each and every one of the superlambananas during the 10 weeks.

There is enough anecdotal and written evidence to suggest that *Go Superlambananas* was, indeed, a unifying experience and that many people's engagement with the event went beyond the appreciation of public art. It provided everyone with the opportunity to respond with their own personal sense of creativity, from storytelling, drawing and colouring to photography and debate and – just as importantly – to have fun.

Special thanks go to Liverpool Culture Company and Northwest Regional Development Agency, who shared our vision to create this truly inspiring event as a highlight of the European Capital of Culture summer programme.

We hope that, like us, many of you will have special memories of those 10 weeks one summer when the superlambananas put a technicolour smile on the face of the city.

From idea to reality: superlambananas are go

The planning behind *Go Superlambananas* began to take shape about 18 months before any of the decorated beasts appeared on the streets. Tim Crutchley, joint MD at advertising agency Finch, was introduced to Wild in Art at the start of the project. He says: 'We'd already worked on the Capital of Culture brand and we knew that a major part of the success of the year would be to get local people involved – to make sure that people in Liverpool got something out of it. It was immediately obvious that *Go Superlambananas* had great potential. It was a fantastic opportunity for the city's communities and it really could touch everybody.'

Finch was tasked with designing and creating the *Go Superlambananas* brand, as a tool both to engage the public and persuade sponsors on board. 'When we created the logo,' Tim continued, 'we wanted to reflect that public interest, to create a balance between the professional artist who'd be involved and the communities, making it obvious that it was something for people of all abilities.'

Sally-Ann and the Wild in Art team had begun the task of knocking on doors, spreading the word and trying to get people involved. 'It was important that we had a mixture of companies and organisations involved,' says Sally. 'I wanted

a spread, from multinationals and SMEs to not-for-profit companies and community groups, and that's what we got. Each meeting we had, from BT and Alliance & Leicester to the TUC and the housing associations, was different. They each had different aims.

'There were so many positives – there were a lot of people out there looking for a way to engage in Capital of Culture and this gave them a way in. It was a way to play a part in the 08 celebrations and an opportunity to think creatively. Although some were first-time sponsors of the arts they ran projects for employees or took on a community project. Some initially felt they were taking a risk, but they all embraced it – there was such a sense of civic pride in Liverpool that they wanted to get involved.'

As the sponsors got involved, the map began to take shape. A key aim for Wild in Art was to put the superlambananas at the heart of the communities that had created them. A trail emerged... Sally-Ann continues: 'I wanted to cover as many of the five boroughs as possible – and the tourist spots too. We wanted some at the waterfront, a flock on Hope Street – we wanted people to see the whole city. I wanted to show, too, that art could be an economic driver

OPPORTUNITY KNOCKS →

REAL SCARF

TEXTURED HAIR
REAL SPECS

REAL BOOTS?

BAA-NITEZ
08

– and I'm sure that the shopping centres would tell you that it drew lots of people in.'

Finch created the map that was to become the definitive map of Merseyside for the summer. 'We started creating it once all of the sponsors and names were in place,' says Tim. 'It was very close to the launch, but a very important piece of the jigsaw.' Merseytravel produced the maps and 200,000 were printed in all, plus thousands of others downloaded from the *Go Superlambananas* website.

And, finally, it was time for the superlambananas to hit the streets. A team of 20 people worked purely on the event's logistics. Liverpool 2020, which takes responsibility for what's known as 'public realm' in Liverpool – the streets and areas we travel around – helped plan the installation of the lambies in their chosen sites. It then took six building contractors: WT Jenkins, Wrenco, Kier, DCT Civil Engineering, Balfour Beatty and Aggregate Industries to install them.

As the next 250 pages show, the results were pretty spectacular…

Go Superlambananas

125 multi-coloured sculptures; 30,000 mosaic tiles; 400 litres of paint; 100 artists; 26 community groups; one escaped lambie and a ransom note. It was quite a spectacle…

Where are they now?

Super 'WiFi' Lambananafon

'Superlambs are brill!
Boss!
Amazin!
Gonna miss you lambies!'

Paige, taken from the Comments Book,
Go Superlambananas display, St George's Plateau, September 8 - 9

Artists - Jon Wood and Gareth Shuttleworth, Chimp Creative
Sponsor - BT FON
Location - ACC, Kings Dock

Sushi, Lamb Tempurabanana
Table 5 now!!

*'Go Superlambananas was
the daftest and best idea of 2008.
I wish we had thought of it. I look
forward to a big reunion next
year – but we'll have to find a
Supersheepdogbanana first.'*

David Fleming
Director
National Museums Liverpool

Artist - Linda Barlow
Sponsor - Sapporo Teppanyaki
Location - ACC, Kings Dock

Lamb-bassador

Artist - Designed by Anna Povall, produced by Benjamin Small
Sponsor - World Firefighters Games 2008
Location - ACC, Kings Dock

Superchromebanana

You can take a horse to water, sorry wrong beast — rather you can take a superlambanana to the waterfront but it still won't drink. But the creature located outside Jurys Inn on Kings Dock found itself the centre of attraction from stars appearing at the nearby Echo Arena during the Summer Pops. Indeed, the word on the street is that Meat Loaf thought he was at a rodeo and mounted the terrified beast!

Artist - Designed by Stephen Heaton, Lawn Creative
Produced by Lloyds Autobody
Sponsor - Jurys Inn
Location - Jurys Inn, Kings Waterfront

SuperSgtPepperYellowLambSubmarineBanana

Artist - Paul McKay
Sponsor - Alliance & Leicester Commercial Bank
Location - Albert Dock

United Lambanana

*'What a wonderful thing this
has been, conjuring up conversation
between all ages. It's been a great
experience. Our family will
miss them dearly.'*

Sharon, Michael, Luke and Harrison, taken from the Comments Book,
Go Superlambananas display, St George's Plateau, September 8 - 9

Artist - Ilsa Parry with Rachael Teare
Sponsor - United Utilities
Location - Albert Dock

Ewes Water Wisely

Artist - Ilsa Parry with Christian Ewen
Sponsor - United Utilities
Location - Albert Dock

Portraits

*'We've had hoards of
people who fly down in taxis,
jump out, have their photos taken with
the superlambanana and then shoot
on to the next one. It's turned into
a massive treasure hunt...'*

Kevin Peacock
Security Guard
Albert Dock

Artist - Clair Freeman
Sponsor - WT Jenkins
Location - Albert Dock

Light Exposure, Light Emission

'It was a fantastic experience auctioning to such a willing crowd. It's not often an auctioneer sells 100% of lots offered, but not only did we achieve that staggering feat but it was interspersed with some spectacular bidding throughout the evening. On at least three occasions, the winning bidder was greeted with a standing ovation. If only that happened at a regular property auction.'

Andrew Binstock
Auctioneer
Sutton Kersh

Artist - Smiling Wolf
Sponsor - Balfour Beatty Civil Engineering
Location - The Strand

Banana Rock

Over the 10 weeks of Go Superlambananas more than 200,000 maps showing where the wee creatures could be found were printed for those keen to get on their trail.

Artist - Christine O'Reilly Wilson
Sponsor - Aggregate Industries
Location - The Strand

Reflectana

Artist - Annabel Wakefield
Sponsor - Kier Construction
Location - Debenhams, Liverpool One

Loop of Life

Artist - Mike Curtis
Sponsor - Crowne Plaza Hotels and Resorts
Location - Crowne Plaza, Princes Dock

Atlambtic Companion

Artist - Nicola McGovern
Sponsor - Atlantic Container Line
Location - Princes Dock

Twinkle

'Lambtastic!'

Glyn, Sue, Jack and Laura, taken from the Comments Book,
Go Superlambananas display, St George's Plateau, September 8 - 9

Artist - the Langhorne family
Sponsor - Malmaison
Location - Malmaison, Princes Dock

SuperPlazaLambanana

Artist - Kate Bedford
Sponsor - Bruntwood
Location - The Plaza, Old Hall Street

THE PLAZA

BRUNTWOOD

Pastures New Super office space from Bruntwood

For more information call 0151 236 1647

Pastures New Super office space from Bruntwood

For more information call 0151 236 1647

SuperChaiseLongueBanana

Artist - Designed by Leanne Wookey, Team a go-go
Produced by J&A Upholstery and Julian J Taylor
Sponsor - Bruntwood
Location - Radisson SAS Hotel, Old Hall Street

Savio the Superlambanana

Eight year 11 students at business and enterprise college Savio in Bootle were responsible for the design of their superlambanana. Sam Briscoe, Jamie Clarkson, Ryan Ferguson, Sarah Humphray, Antonia Johnson, Lyndsey O'Rourke, Emily Rebic and Katy Tyson designed and painted Savio with the help of Cumbria-based artist Kerry Hunt.

The eight art students decorated their superlambanana with their vision of the future of business in Liverpool, including coins, pie charts, the city's skyline and footballs. Emily says: 'We all had a go at drawing different designs, and then we picked out the bits we liked and the artist drew them onto our superlambanana.

'We weren't allowed to put a Savio school tie on it,' she says, 'but Kerry said we could put our names on, so we all came in the next morning before it was varnished and put our names on one foot. Then I read on the internet somewhere that someone had written "hopefully all the names'll get scrubbed off", which made me laugh!'

Savio partner, Alliance & Leicester, asked the school to decorate one of the two lambs they'd sponsored. Lyndsey said: 'it was a new thing for all of us. And I'd love to do it again. Designing was the best bit – it took us about an hour and a half to design it, and then we had to finish it that day.'

The Savio students combined visiting their finished superlambanana with a cultural trip around the city centre, taking in the Maritime Museum and Albert Dock. It also encouraged them to get involved in seeing the rest of the lambies dotted across Merseyside.

It's undoubtedly an experience the Savio students won't forget. 'It's a good thing to put on my CV' says Sarah, and the team took great pride in sending their friends and family to see their superlambanana at the heart of Liverpool's business district, in St Paul's Square: 'My mum was made up,' says Emily. 'She was like a kid at Christmas when she saw it!'

**Artist - Kerry Hunt and business students
from Savio High School
Sponsor - Alliance & Leicester Commercial Bank
Location - St Paul's Square, Old Hall Street**

Commercial District Skyline

Artist - David Fanning
Sponsor - Liverpool Commercial District Partnership
Location - St Paul's Square, Old Hall Street

Mona

An astonishing sum of £550,000 was raised by the sale of nearly 70 superlambananas at a charity auction held at St George's Hall — double what was expected, making it the most successful ever charity fund raiser on Merseyside.

Artist - Charlotte Brown
Sponsor - English Cities Fund
Location - St Paul's Square, Old Hall Street

Supergrassbanana

The grass covered Supergrassbanana, located in the city's business quarter in Old Hall Street, sold for £20,000, a tad over the £6,000 expected!

Artist - Designed by Stephen Heaton, Lawn Creative
Produced by Julian J Taylor
Sponsor - Hill Dickinson Lawyers
Location - Old Hall Street

Baa-ve New World

Artist - Sally Olding
Sponsor - Liverpool Vision
Location - Town Hall, Castle Street

SuperCottonwoolbanana

Artist - Kate Bedford
Sponsor - Bruntwood
Location - Cotton Exchange, Old Hall Street

SuperLoveBanana

'I love ewe all, please come back next year.'

Helen McDonald, taken from the Comments Book
at Superlambanana display St George's Plateau, September 8 - 9

Artist - Anna Benson
Sponsor - Liverpool Registration Service
Location - Cotton Exchange Courtyard

Superlambbananaleaves

Artist - Alison Little
Sponsor - Brock Carmichael Architects,
BCA Landscape and BCA Project Services
Location - Cotton Exchange, Old Hall Street

First Past the Post

*'These are the modern day Liver Birds!!
What a great icon for our great city.'*

Taken from the Comments Book,
Go Superlambananas display, St George's Plateau, September 8 - 9

Artist - Pamela Holstein
Sponsor - Liverpool Chamber of Commerce and Industry
Location - Number One, Old Hall Street

SuperLawbanana

'As a leading Liverpool law firm, it was very apt for us to sponsor SuperLawbanana and Supergrassbanana as they provided hundreds of passers-by with a fantastic photo opportunity outside our new headquarters on Old Hall Street.'

Tony Wilson
Senior Partner
Hill Dickinson LLP

**Artist - Clare Gammond and Jeanne-Marie Kenny
Sponsor - Hill Dickinson Lawyers**

Top Banana

Artist - Finch and Candida Boyes
Sponsor - Rumford Investments
Location - 20 Chapel Street

Rocksy

*'Cumbria has been celebrating
Year of Adventure in 2008 so we wanted
an idea to promote it, but also wanted to take
inspiration from Cumbria's outstanding natural
beauty. A tactile, rugged approach was taken
in the design of Rocksy to illustrate the area's
contribution to outdoor activities and the
inspiring mountainous landscape.'*

Catherine Caswell worked with regional artists
to design Rocksy on behalf of the NWDA

Artist - Ben Cook
Sponsor - Northwest Regional Development Agency
Location - Exchange Flags

Chops

'Chops is a nod towards Taste Lancashire 08, but also illustrates the quirky humour of the region with an homage to the traditional illustration used by butchers, but featuring a colourful modern twist.'

Designer Steve Kerner worked with regional artists
on behalf of the NWDA

Artist - Alix Dryden
Sponsor - Northwest Regional Development Agency
Location - Exchange Flags

Flora

'Cheshire is a beautiful place renowned for its many stunning and varied gardens. Flora was designed with Cheshire's Year of Gardens 08 and the county's proud garden heritage in mind.'

Howard Fox helped to design Flora
working with regional artists on behalf of the NWDA

Artist - Rosalind Hargreaves
Sponsor - Northwest Regional Development Agency
Location - Exchange Flags

B of the Baa

'B of the Baa features an athletics track in honour of Manchester's tremendous Year of World Sport 08. The North West is a region which is passionate about sport and has made a huge contribution towards sport, so I wanted to reflect that.'

Designer Steve Kerner worked with regional artists on behalf of the NWDA

Artist - Phil Costello
Sponsor - Northwest Regional Development Agency
Location - Exchange Flags

Superlordmayorlambanana

'The lambananas must stay....or the city will riot!!!!'

Taken from the Comments Book,
Go Superlambananas display, St George's Plateau, September 8 - 9

Artist - Brian Hanlon
Sponsor - Liverpool City Council
Location - Town Hall

SuperRoyalambanana

'At its worst Liverpool's essence is scallies,
scams and stuck in the past. At its best Liverpool's
essence is passion, excitement, ideas and a certain coolness.
Currently the Liver Bird is the symbol of the city. Is the Liver Bird
the best symbol for the future? A Liver Bird represents a Liverpool
of times long ago. I'd argue that it's time to move on. We have just
seen unprecedented public interest in a new, iconic and cool
symbol – the superlambanana. Why not take the bull
by the horns and make this innovative
sculpture our new city emblem?'

David De Maestri
Chartered Marketeer and Master Coach
in the Liverpool Daily Post, October 2008

Artist - Kate Bedford
Sponsor - Bruntwood
Location - Queens Arcade, Castle Street

Lambline

Artist - Rachael Ward
Sponsor - Merseytravel
Location - James Street Station

Sgt Pepper

*'When you think of
Liverpool and Merseyside
you inevitably think of the Beatles.
I thought John Lennon's unique talent
and personality was ideal to represent
Liverpool during its year as the
European Capital of Culture.'*

Paul Fox

**Artist - Fine art and design students, Liverpool Hope University
Sponsor - Hard Day's Night Hotel
Location - Blakes Restaurant, North John Street**

Superlambgranada

Ken Tinsley bought the Superlambgranada lambie in the online auction, which took place just days after the live auction in St George's Hall. 'Ours has all the North West place names splattered all over it,' he says. 'We wanted something that was identifiable as being Liverpool or North West-based, and Superlambgranada was probably our second choice. And it has the bonus of having a transport connection – we run a small transport company.

'We had an eye on the Supermapbanana, which features south Liverpool road names, including the roads where both Richard (my brother and business partner) and I live. But it was the last on the online auction list and we were worried that we'd get priced out – and we were right, it went for £6,200 – so we decided to go for the Granada one.

'I've never bought anything costing more than £50 before, and only on eBay,' Ken admits. 'We were hoping to spend about £3,000, but went up to £3,200 (plus VAT) to secure our superlambie. We were chuffed to bits... It was a pretty tense couple of hours as the auction went on – not much work

was done that day! We put a bid in with 20 seconds to go and I believe just pipped Granada, the original sponsor.

'We're hoping to put the superlamb in our new office, although that will be some way off. At the moment it's sitting in my dining room, but you can see plenty of people walking past stopping and smiling when they see it.'

For the Tinsleys too, it was something the whole family got involved in – the idea for buying a superlambanana first came up as the family hit the trail over the summer. Ken says: 'We took our kids (Alex, nine and Eva, six) around the city to see various superlambananas and they loved them – they probably saw 50 or 60. I think *Go Superlambananas* has been one of the real successes of 2008 – it managed to involve a lot of different groups in designing them in the first place, and seems to be the one event that has had universal acclaim in Liverpool without any moans... You know – too elitist, too crowded, too expensive, didn't start exactly on time, etc, etc. We do like to moan!'

Artist - Mark Nuttall
Sponsor - ITV Granada
Location - Liverpool One

Reports
REPORTING YOUR STORIES
THE DESIGNERS YOU LOVE AR
COMING
ROCKFERRY
ADSWOOD
GISBURN
BASHALL EAVES
BROCKHALL
CRANK
PRESCOT
DUNHAM-ON-THE-HILL
CHORLEY
GARSTON
BOLD
WIDNES
MOSSLEY
DUTTON
FLEETWOOD
BOOTLE
CROXTETH
CRAWSHAWBOOTH
WORSTHORNE
TABLEY
SUPERIOR
BRUERA
BUDWORTH
MOULDSWORTH
ASTON by
WATERFOOT
CANNING
RAINHILL
EDGE HILL
THORNTON
NETHERTON
ORRELL PARK
HAYDOCK
MIDDLEWICH
TATTENHALL
WEAVERHAM
SAUGHALL MASSIE
ALLITHWAITE
PRESTBURY
RUNCORN
SMITHY BRIDGE
WYBUNBURY
FOULRIDGE
HELMSHORE
COLNE
SANDBACH
HALE BARNS
POULTON
FAILSWORTH
BILLINGTON
NORTH RODE
SIDDINGTON
SWETTENHAM
CLAYTON-le-WOODS
SILVERDALE
EDENFIELD
CLITHEROE
GOOSNARGH
MILNROW
BLACKPOOL
GRIZEBECK
NETHER KELLET
LANCASTER
SEAFORTH
MELLOR
GANTSFIELD
HALEWOOD
BACKFORD
HESWALL
THORNTON HOUGH
VAUXHALL
RUFFORD
ABRAM
WRAY
TABLEY
BROXTON
LITTLEBOROUGH
SCALES
ARCLID
NETHER
SIMISTER
SEDGWICK
DOLPHINHOLME
LEDSHAM
ULVERSTON
SPEKE
BURGH
LACEY GREEN
BURNLEY
WINDLE
TATTLESHULME
GAWSWORTH
ASHLEY
OVER ALDERLEY
BOLLINGTON
OAKENSHAW

Superconnectedlambanana

'Great boost for the morale of Liverpool'

Val Smith, taken from the Comments Book,
Go Superlambananas display, St George's Plateau, September 8 - 9

Artist - Alison Little
Sponsor - BT Openzone Wireless Broadband
Location - BHS, Lord Street

Pete Price's Super Laugh Banana

'These lambs have
put a HUGE grin on my face
every time I see them!
You've brought Liverpool
closer together.
THANKYOU!'

Taken from the Comments Book,
Go Superlambananas display, St George's Plateau, September 8 - 9

Artist - Created by Pete Price
Designed and produced by Phillip Marsden
Sponsor - Liverpool Daily Post and Echo
Location - Metquarter

I Love Granadaland

Artist - Laura McCreesh and Mike Badger
Sponsor - ITV Granada Reports
Location - Metquarter

Baa-Nitez

By the time thoughts turned to creating individual lambies, advertising agency Finch had already been asked to create the *Go Superlambananas* identity and trail map – and superlambananaitis was running at fever pitch throughout the agency. 'We were desperate to design our very own superlambanana, so decided to run an internal competition, giving everybody the chance to create a superlambanana that would really engage with people,' says joint MD, Tim Crutchley. 'Everyone in the agency came up with some fantastic concepts and we all had a lot of fun along the way.

'The winning idea of Baa-Nitez was a concept that really resonated – Liverpool is a city that's synonymous with sport and football is at its very heart… Baa-Nitez was the idea we all voted for – even our resident bluenoses gave it the thumbs up.'

So, Baa-Nitez was born and, on 19 May, got to meet his namesake at Liverpool's training ground, Melwood. He was born to stardom – the next day stealing the headlines as he appeared on the front pages of the Liverpool Daily Post and numerous nationals.

'The replica Baa-Nitez is a great idea and a lot of fun,' said the real Rafa. But, as Jamie Carragher toured the superlambananas to suss them out in advance of the auction, he was asked if he'd be stumping up the cash to bid for Rafa Baa-Nitez. 'I can't have the Rafa one,' he said. 'If he had a go at me after a match I'd go home and kick it.'

Artist - Designed by Dave Thomas, Finch – the ideas agency
Produced by Candida Boyes
Sponsor - Finch
Location - Metquarter

Petite Fleur

Artist - Helene-Marie Gilmour
Sponsor - Metquarter
Location - Metquarter

Superfitbanana

'Provided an excellent health tour
— got people walking and talking'

Taken from the Comments Book,
Go Superlambananas display, St George's Plateau, September 8 - 9

Artist - Shape Design
Sponsor - Lifestyles Fitness Centres
Location - Millennium House, Whitechapel

SuperWagBagBanana

'We were approached by Liverpool BID to work on their superlambanana and asked to come up with a concept based on shopping, as they look after the city centre retailers. We combined shopping with our specialist area - luxury leather handbags – and came up with the idea of combining our speciality, a handbag, with a 'WAG' – as they're often renowned for the expensive designer handbags they carry.

We worked with local artist/illustrator John McNally and came up with the idea of turning the superlambanana into a giant handbag! We went through loads of ideas – some of which were a bit over the top, some we decided wouldn't survive the weather – and finally decided to go with something simple...We wanted to keep it sleek and not too obvious, so by painting it high sheen black, to look like patent leather, and adding gold chain handles, gold whip-stitching effect and finishing it off with a giant gold zip down its back, we transformed it into the SuperWagBagBanana.

Nina Halliwell
Nook & Willow

Artist - Nook & Willow with John McNally
Sponsor - Liverpool City Central Business
Improvement District
Location - Houghton Street

Koppy

Other highlights of the auction included the Koppy superlambanana, inspired by Liverpool FC's new strip and signed by the players, which sold for £12,000, a fair hike on its guide price of £7,000.

Artist - Graham Berry, the Apple Agency
Sponsor - Adidas
Location - LFC Shop, Liverpool One

Homer

Also lashing out the cash was Big Brother winner Craig Phillips — a born and bred Scouser who is now a property developer and builder, oh and television personality. He snapped up the Homer sculpture — which was kitted out in working clothes — for £10,000, double the expected figure.

'My heart was set on Homer as it represents the building industry.'

**Artist - Kim Tan, Creative Services, Liverpool City Council
Sponsor - Liverpool Mutual Homes with Fusion 21
Location - Wellington Column, Lime Street**

Our Working Community

*'A cross between a lamb
and a banana – that's
typical Liverpool. Anything
that brings fun, laughter
and joy to Liverpool
is worth supporting.'*

Ken Dodd
Backing the Liverpool Daily Post
campaign to save SuperLambBanana for the city

Artist - Holly Langley
Sponsor - North West TUC
Location - Wellington Column, St George's Plateau

Monument to the Superlambanana

'The Monument to the Superlambanana adopts the style and proportions of an equestrian statue, and we hoped that having the sculpture outside the World Museum would draw attention to the city's many historic public monuments.'

David Fleming
Director
National Museums Liverpool

Artist - Andrew Jackson
Sponsor - Public Monuments and Sculpture Association
Location - World Museum, William Brown Street

Superfive-a-daybanana

*'I remember rustling up a
recipe for lamb banana stew in the
Echo as a bit of a jape to publicise the
sculpture and Lewis Biggs tells me
it was that dish that got a lot of people
interested and excited
in the whole project.'*

Joe Riley
Arts Editor
Liverpool Echo

**Artist - Vince Cleghorne and Kensington Junior Youth Inclusion Project
Sponsor - National Museums Liverpool
Location - Walker Art Gallery, William Brown Street**

SuperLightBanana

'Thank you for the magic'

Rhodie Blythe, Liverpool, taken from the Comments Book,
Go Superlambananas display, St George's Plateau, September 8 - 9

Artist - Lisa Rostron, Lawn Creative
Produced by Julian J Taylor
Sponsor - 2020 Liverpool
Location - St George's Hall Visitor Centre

Cargo

*'Lovely for us from New Zealand.
Thank you. We have 4,000,000 people
and 20,000,000 lambs.'*

Taken from the Comments Book,
Go Superlambananas display, St George's Plateau, September 8 - 9

Artist - Phillip Marsden
Sponsor - St George's Hall, Liverpool City Council
Location - St George's Hall Visitor Centre

Our George

'There's another of those bananaramas…'

Passer-by
Lime Street

Artist - Liverpool 08 Volunteers & KECS Creative Community Arts
Sponsor - 08 Welcome Liverpool Culture Company
Location - St George's Plateau

Superlambananatree

'Go Superlambananas
*was one of the most exciting
parts of Capital of Culture year.
It was just pure joy and sunshine.
Everywhere you went it made
you smile and it was accessible
to everyone.'*

Angela Heslop
Arts Editor
BBC Radio Merseyside

**Artist - Amanda Oliphant
Sponsor - Virgin Trains
Location - Lime Street Station**

Baa Baa Braille Sheep

Baa Baa Braille Sheep
Have you any dots?
Yes Sir, Yes Sir
Lots and lots

One for the Liverbirds
One for the Docks
And the rest for the people
Who read the dots

**Artist - Jola Kurzeja-Ryan with children
from the National Blind Children's Society
Sponsor - Merseytravel
Location - Lime Street Station**

Green Lamb

Cartoonist and photographer Tony Hall, syndication manager at Trinity Mirror's offices in Liverpool, picked up first prize in the company's 08 Creative Awards. His witty yet provocative photomontage image replaced the Liver Birds atop the Royal Liver Building with two 'lambananas', winning in the individual arts section. The competition was launched to celebrate Liverpool's European Capital of Culture year and to seek out talented and artistic people who work for Trinity Mirror across the Merseyside region.

Artist - Designed by Ed Butler
Produced by Julian J Taylor
Sponsor - Holiday Inn Hotels and Resorts
Location - Holiday Inn, Lime Street

Friendship Forever

'A wonderful idea – I found 61 of them on the superlambanana trail and am seeing the rest of them today. It's promoting friendliness as well. I've met and chatted with loads of people. Congratulations Wild in Art, congratulations Liverpool!'

Moelyne Hammond, Newtown, Powys, taken from the Comments Book, *Go Superlambananas* display, St George's Plateau, September 8 - 9

Artist - Designed by Jessica Gardiner
Produced by Benjamin Small
Sponsor - St John's Shopping Centre
Location - St John's Shopping Centre Café

Push Me Pull Ewe

*'Personally I am not that fond of it
as a piece of art but if it encourages
young people to have a go then I am all
for it. Anything which attracts visitors
to the city has got to be a good thing
— and I would gladly keep it if we could
wave goodbye to the Mersey wave.'*

Paul Flanagan
Owner of the Newz Bar and Sir Thomas Hotel
on the fight to keep SuperLambBanana in Liverpool

Artist - Phillip Marsden
Produced by Ben Cook
Sponsor - Sayers the Bakers
Location - St John's Shopping Centre

Beryl Sebastian

Natalie Gornell was one of four teenagers who designed and painted Youngaddaction's Beryl Sebastian superlambanana, alongside Michaela Jones, Chrissie Connors, Ben Parker, other members of the Youngaddaction Advisory Group and artists Sophie Backhouse and Ian Town.

Youngaddaction Liverpool is a drug and alcohol treatment charity, supporting young people in Liverpool who have issues with drugs and alcohol as well as offering support to family and relatives who may also be affected. Natalie says: 'My mum used to work at Addaction and she got me involved. Our superlambanana's called Beryl Sebastian because the girls wanted a girl's name, but to make it fair for Ben we said he could choose a boy's name as well and we just joined them together,' explains the 14-year-old.

Beryl Sebastian's design includes historical and cultural events, including the Dockers' Strike, Blitz, football and music connections. 'We all worked together on it and put our ideas together before we decided what worked and what didn't,' Natalie

says. Like her female/ male name, Beryl Sebastian's design is firmly split down the middle, with a darker, patched-up historical side, and a lighter, brighter contemporary side. 'But,' says Natalie, 'my favourite part's definitely the modern colourful skyline side. I really enjoyed it, but if I did it again I would like more people to help and more time. It was a really hard day's work!'

As with each of the 125 superlambananas, everyone you speak to has a different opinion on the best. 'I didn't go round all of them, as they were all over the place,' admits Natalie. 'But – apart from Beryl Sebastian – I really like the one which was placed on the roundabout by Speke, it's peeled like a banana. And I like the one in a suit too.'

The St George's Hall charity auction became the highest ever fundraiser on Merseyside and an unforgettable night for anyone who was there. Beryl Sebastian was sold for £6,500. 'I think we've done really well,' says Natalie, 'and I'm very proud.'

**Artist - Youngaddaction Liverpool Youth Advisory Group,
Sophie Backhouse and Ian Town
Sponsor - Youngaddaction Liverpool
Location - Clayton Square**

24hoursuperlambanana

'We saw the first original in 1998
before emigrating to Oz and returned
to see all of them today. Don't let them
emigrate out of Liverpool.'

Ann and Tony, Bootle, taken from the Comments Book,
Go Superlambananas display, St George's Plateau, September 8 - 9

Artist - Debbie Ryan
Sponsor - 08 Business Connect
Location - Clayton Square

SuperLewis'sLamb 152

Artist - Lewis's In-house Visual Team
Sponsor - Lewis's
Location - Lewis's Department Store, Ranelagh Street

Working Towards the Future

'Please keep the lamb or we will cry'

Joseph, age 3 and Alex, age 2, taken from the Comments Book, *Go Superlambananas* display, St George's Plateau, September 8 - 9

Artist - Mike Badger with pupils from St Matthew's and St Mary's RC Primary Schools
Sponsor - Pertemps People Development Group
Location - Church Street

Lamsa

Artist - Katriona Beales, Finoon Saleh and 10 young winners of the Shine competition
Sponsor - The Bluecoat
Location - Bluecoat Courtyard

Fire Cracker to Martian Skies

'We have always done well with superlambananas — we've sold the miniature ones for years and they've always been extremely popular,' says Dick Mawdsley, co-owner of Utility on Bold Street. 'Then we were approached by Wild in Art to have a couple of the superlambananas in our window early on, as a pre-launch for the event. Laurence Payot's Fire Cracker to Martian Skies were beautiful — brilliant design. Bright and colourful, just like the shop. We don't do beige here.'

The response, according to Dick, was unlike anything they'd ever done before: 'There's just so much enthusiasm for them,' he says. 'And from completely unlikely people...The response has been crazy and there's been so much goodwill. I'd say that having them in the window has trebled our footfall, and sales of the ceramic miniatures, micro-lambs and colouring books went through the roof.

'I think the sculpture works because it has both meaning and humour. There's a story behind it, and all summer you'd hear people asking, "What's this thing I keep seeing?" As a comment on Liverpool's

trading past — and, of course, genetic engineering — it has meaning in our dumbed-down culture. But I just love hearing what people call them when they come in; they ask for the camel dog, for cats, for dogs. But my favourite was the superlamborghini!'

Everyone, it seems, had his or her own superlambanana story to tell. 'We had a grandmother come in looking for the small ceramic models,' continues Dick. 'She was terminally ill, but had spent the summer taking her grandsons around 60 or so of the superlambananas, and she wanted to give them each a superlambanana to remember her by. We were struggling to get our hands on them, but we managed to get some for her.

'As an event it's just blown everything out of the water, and I love the fact that they were so successful in Liverpool — I think three times as much money was raised at the auction than in Manchester, which is astonishing.' And, with prices for the Martian skyrocketing at auction, I asked Dick if Utility were not keen to keep their beloved superlambananas? 'We were tempted,' says Dick. 'But not that tempted!'

Artist - Laurence Payot
Sponsor - Utility
Location - Bold Street

The Loving Lamb

*'Loved the
superlambananas —
this was truly a cultural event
which everyone embraced.
I wish they could stay.'*

Taken from the Comments Book,
Go Superlambananas display, St George's Plateau, September 8 - 9

Artist - Annemarie Read
Sponsor - Greater Merseyside Learning Providers Federation
Location - Berry Street

The Rope Walker

'Excellent idea —
another animal next year!
It inspired the imagination.'

Taken from the Comments Book,
Go Superlambananas display, St George's Plateau, September 8 - 9

Artist - Designed and produced by BDP and Shape Design
Sponsor - BDP
Location - St Peter's Square

Yellow Superlambanana in a cage. 2008

We didn't just want to decorate a superlambanana, we wanted to bring it to life... create an experience,' says Uniform MD Nick Howe of their interactive lambie, Yellow Superlambanana in a Cage. The superlambanana was the star of a story that evolved over 10 weeks, starting life caged in Arthouse Square, before her escape, subsequent recapture at Albert Dock and her eventual release into the wild on Crosby beach.

'We wanted to support the event, and at the same time do something that the whole company could get behind,' says Nick. 'We started by looking at the notion of a live creature – examining it like Damien Hirst did with his shark in formaldehyde and it grew out of that...' Uniform's digital department got involved, animating the iconic beast and creating between 30 and 40 sequences to make the three news pieces, with 10 –15 clips making up each story.

Granada Reports broadcast three news pieces on the 'only superlambanana in captivity' and, in the studio, presenters Tony Morris and Lucy Meacock provided links for the superlambanana stories. Reporter Matt O'Donoghue, who fronted the three news pieces, takes over the story: 'We'd talked about using the Granada brand on the web virals, but my boss suggested doing it for real – as a news item on the show – which gave the whole thing a sense of authenticity. So we worked up the storyboard, creating a whole backstory: feeding the superlambanana, having it escape and finally releasing it into the wild. The response we got from viewers was overwhelming. Well over a million people saw it, and we had comments ranging from "how do they do it?" to "we're sorry to hear it's escaped..."'

Tamsin Valentino, Uniform's client services manager was in charge of the PR and very active in watching the response to the story. 'When she escaped we had a team out in town handing out 'missing' flyers – the response was huge. People really took it to their hearts, leaving reports of sightings on our blog...' Nick says: 'The idea was to get as many people as possible involved in the story. Granada got us a huge audience... People were totally convinced!'

Developers Iliad bought Yellow Superlambanana in a Cage and she's back on the streets of Liverpool, in the East Village. With any luck, she won't escape this time...

Artist - Uniform
Sponsor - Uniform
Location - Arthouse Square

Deerlamboltnana

Artist - T J Dolan (Krek)
Sponsor - Wild in Art
Location - East Village, Duke Street

Art Vandelist

'I must admit I was hugely tickled by SuperLambBanana. It has rapidly become an integral part of Liverpool's public art arena and is now almost regarded as the 21st *century symbol of the city, while the Liver Birds maybe look to the past.'*

Stephen Broadbent
Sculptor and former student of
Liverpool artist Arthur Dooley

Artist - Artvandelay.com
Sponsor - PS Collective
Location - East Village, Duke Street

The Best of British

'Superlambanana sounds revolting, silly and rude. What the hell has it got to do with Liverpool?'

Jean Boht
Actress and star of the Liverpool-based
Bread television comedy series

Artist - Mark Garrod
Sponsor - Cains
Location - Cains Brewery

Twinnylambanana

Did you know that more than 20 different ceramic replicas of the original SuperLambBanana were produced for fans to collect? They included the Super Cow Banana, the Super Choconana, and a Capital of Culture-themed version.

Artist - Young People from the Partner Cities of Dublin and Liverpool with KECS Creative Community Arts
Sponsor - European Year of Intercultural Dialogue, Liverpool Culture Company
Location - Hope Street

Herd Days Night

Artist - Mark Jones
Sponsor - Maghull Developments
Location - Hope Street

Purple Sky At Night

*'I love
SuperLambBanana as a work
of sculpture – it's Mickey Mouse
out of Henry Moore.
It is a fun, modern icon
for Liverpool.'*

Phil Key
Arts Editor
Liverpool Daily Post

Artist - Alex Jackson
Sponsor - Wrenco
Location - Hope Street

BackBitternBanana, BackBitternBanana.com

Artist - Sophie Bower and Kathryn Pattullo
Sponsor - Liverpool School of Art & Design, Liverpool John Moores University
Location - Metropolitan Cathedral Plaza

SuperStudentlambanana

Artist - Jeanne-Marie Kenny
Sponsor - University of Liverpool
Location - Brownlow Hill

Superabbeyroadbanana

'Awesome!
From Texas.'

Taken from the Comments Book,
Go Superlambananas display, St George's Plateau, September 8 - 9

Artist - Vince Cleghorne and the Kensington Youth Inclusion Project
Sponsor - Kier North West
Location - Brownlow Hill

Zip

Artist - Janice Egerton
Sponsor - Liverpool Hope University
Location - The Cornerstone Building

Superkalazarbanana

The Liverpool School of Tropical Medicine sponsored the SuperKalazarBanana as an artistic interpretation of its work into the tropical disease Leishmaniasis, and it even has a Facebook following. And, rather ironically, the famous Liverpool shipowner Sir Alfred Lewis Jones imported and popularised the banana as a nutritional source of food for the working classes – and was a founder of the School of Tropical Medicine in 1899.

Artist - Ektor Diaz and Rod Dillon
Sponsor - Liverpool School of Tropical Medicine
Location - Pembroke Place

Kenny the Superlamb

Artist - Barbara Galt and children from the local area
Sponsor - City and North Neighbourhood Managment Services
Location - Hall Lane, Kensington

It's Just a Superlambanana

Writer Alan Bleasdale reckoned that the late Liverpool sculptor Arthur Dooley, who created many works of public art, would have railed at the superlambanana, even suggesting that if still around he would be leading the march across the Pennines in protest. Others disagreed. Actress Margi Clarke predicted that the sculpture would tickle that famous Scouse sense of humour and joked: 'And at least it's a vegetarian lamb.'

Artist - Harry Harris
Sponsor - Community Justice Centre, North Liverpool
Location - Community Justice Centre, Boundary Street

The North End

'They are the best thing to happen to Liverpool in a long time. They brighten up the terrible summer we had. They made us smile. Please keep them here…'

Michelle Linger, taken from the Comments Book,
Go Superlambananas display, St George's Plateau, September 8 - 9

**Artist - Claire Stringer and pupils from
Trinity RC Primary School
Sponsor - Vauxhall Neighbourhood Council
Location - NSPCC, Great Homer Street**

SuperLarryLambanana

Artist - Mike Badger and pupils from Lawrence Community Primary School
Sponsor - Riverside Group
Location - Picton Children's Centre, Lawrence Road

SuperConeBanana

SuperConeBanana pays tribute to the humble traffic cone — tens of thousands of which took to the streets during Liverpool's Big Dig — the first holes and hold-ups of which happened on the Edge Lane approach to the city. Hence it was a fitting location for SuperConeBanana over the summer of 2008.

Karl Dolan
Open Culture

Artist - Jacqueline Boylan
Sponsor - Open Culture
Location - ICDC, Edge Lane

Stanley

Artist - Vince Cleghorne and pupils from Hugh Baird College
Sponsor - Evolve Neighbourhood Regeneration & Hugh Baird College
Location - Hugh Baird College, Stanley Road

Rocking Superlambanana

Liverpool artist Alex Corina was one of the first to put on show a modified version of the sculpture, which he had transformed into a rocking horse. It was first seen at the opening reception for *Go Superlambananas* at Liverpool's Static gallery in February 2008, which was sponsored by the Liverpool Culture Company. Over 200 guests chuckled at Alex's concept and roared with delight as French-born artist Laurence Payot, who lives in Aigburth but hails from Marly in north-east France, poured brightly coloured paint over two of the sculptures to create a rainbow effect superlambanana. Alex is co-ordinator of the Garston Cultural Village campaign and had once pushed for Garston to be the sculpture's permanent home. He commented: 'The superlambanana has become an icon representing Garston and Liverpool's heritage of exporting lambs and importing bananas that combines both with humour. The other link is that not only was Garston docks the route for exporting lambs and importing bananas, but the sculpture was made in Garston, at the old Bryant and May factory.'

Artist - Alex Corina
Sponsor - Wild in Art and Royal Liverpool Children's Hospital
Alder Hey Imagine Appeal
Location - Royal Liverpool Hospital Alder Hey

'Peekaboo' Newsham Superlambanana

**Artist - AiR Associates: Sharon, Denise, Trisha and Robert
with the communities of north Liverpool
Sponsor - Arts in Regeneration and Newsham
Adult Learning Service
Location - Newsham Park, Newsham Drive**

SuperFanBanana

*'The experience of working
with Liverpool FC community department
on the SLB project was a wonderful experience
for all the pupils of the Royal Liverpool School for
the Blind. This project was a real hands-on
tactile experience and every child had
the opportunity to get involved and
put their own handprint on
the superlambanana.'*

Linda Hogan
Royal Liverpool School for the Blind

**Artist - Steve Rooney, Sue Williams and
Liverpool Royal School for the Blind
Sponsor - Liverpool Football Club
Location - Liverpool Football Club, Anfield Road**

Roy G Biv

*'Locals and tourists
love SuperLambBanana
and to take it out of Liverpool
would be like removing
the Mona Lisa from
the Louvre.'*

Francis McEntegart
Director
Chime Creative Management

**Artist - Olivia Simpson
Sponsor - DCT Civil Engineering
Location - The Strand**

Blueberry Banana

'It took the whole school — 320 children from age 3 to age 11 — to paint our superlambanana. Everyone designed one on A4 paper and Debbie Ryan (a mosaic artist) chose parts from as many as she could to include in the final design. We like the face, community, best city in the world, eye patch, the tail, spotty legs, head, half-beard and flower...'

Representatives from Blueberry Park's School Council
and the Liverpool Schools Parliament

Artist - Debbie Ryan and pupils from Blueberry Park Primary School
Sponsor - Berrybridge Housing Association
Location - Blueberry School, Ackers Hall Avenue

Superbeezbuzzbyawildlambanana

The well-known Indian restaurant Gulshan, located in the south of the city on Aigburth Road, made its own mouth-watering contribution to the Go Superlambananas craze. Owners Mustafa and Salina Rhaman created a special 'Superlambhunana' curry comprising lamb and bananas – what else – all fired with spices and aromatic herbs.

Artist - Jan Bell and Caroline Hunt
Sponsor - HLF Wildflower Heroes Project
Location - National Wildflower Centre

Fazakerley Night Fever

*'Great to see imagination
and simple hand made art
rather than digital images.
Keep them or make more.'*

Taken from the Comments Book,
Go Superlambananas display, St George's Plateau, September 8 - 9

Artist - Vik
Sponsor - Aintree University Hospitals NHS Foundation Trust
Location - Aintree Hospital

Fizz

Artist - Sharon Mutch and Fazakerley 506 Detached Youth Project
Sponsor - Cobalt Housing
Location - Fazakerley Community Federation

Tinky

'Go Superlambananas is a fantastic example of public art which everyone can enjoy and has involved everyone from big business to small community groups — and that's quite an achievement.'

Phil Redmond
Deputy Chairman of the Liverpool Culture Company

**Artist - Neil Keating and the Walton Youth Project at
Alsop High School
Sponsor - Liverpool Housing Trust
Location - Walton-on-the-Hill Church**

Bridge-it

Artist - Louise Wood and Clubmoor Youth Centre
Sponsor - Alt Valley Neighbourhood Management Services
Location - Clubmoor Youth Centre, Larkhill Lane

Superlidbanana
(Black Bull)

*'This couldn't have happened
in any other city in the world.
Only Liverpool could have embraced
the creativity of this event with such
excitement and commitment.'*

Sally-Ann Wilkinson
Director
Wild in Art

Artist - Nicki McCubbing with Orrell Park Youth Club
Sponsor - Alt Valley Neighbourhood Management Services
Location - Black Bull pub, Cedar Road

Cobanana

Artist - Cobalt Youth Board with Andrew Weston
Sponsor - Cobalt Housing
Location - Lower House Lane and Utting Avenue

Super St Domingo Lamb Banana

Artist - Candida Boyes
Sponsor - Everton Football Club
Location - Goodison Park, adjacent to Dixie Dean statue

The Superlambridge

Artist - Joanne Kelly and Emily Lansley
Sponsor - Halton Borough Council
Location - Runcorn Railway Station

Smiley Lamb

'They make everyone smile'

B Greene, Wirral, taken from the Comments Book,
Go Superlambananas display, St George's Plateau, September 8 - 9

Artist - Designed by Alex Austin
Produced by Emily Lansley
Sponsor - Halton Borough Council
Location - Runcorn Railway Station

Youth Division

'Our design was inspired
by the way children label each
other as Goths, Chavs and so on.
We wanted to mix the different cultures
together to show how society in the North
West has grown over the years.'

Pupils at the Wade Deacon High School, who won a competition
to design their own superlambanana

Artist - Wade Deacon Arts Team with Sophie Backhouse and Ian Town
Sponsor - BBC North West Tonight and Arts Council England North West
Location - Speke Boulevard

Peel

*'Development of the "Peel" lambanana
allowed me to create a visual celebration of
the vibrancy, playfulness and humour of
our city and its people.'*

Ilsa Parry
Artist

**Artist - Designed and created by Ilsa Parry
Produced by Ben Cook
Sponsor - The Riverside Group
Location - Speke Boulevard**

Urbananasplash

Artist - Julian J Taylor
Sponsor - Urban Splash
Location - Matchworks

Generation 21

*'They should put one in
each of the cities twinned
with Liverpool!'*

Janet from Woolton, taken from the Comments Book,
Go Superlambananas display, St George's Plateau, September 8 - 9

**Artist - Designed by Toxteth Learning Networks School
Produced by Roz Hyde
Sponsor - Liverpool Healthy Cities
Location - Aigburth Road**

Bloomin Lamb Banana (Petal)

Artist - Art Department of Lower Lee School
Sponsor - Woolton in Bloom, funded by Woolton Educational and Recreational Trust
Location - Woolton Street, Woolton

World Changer

Artist - Hannah Marshall
Sponsor - Frontline Church
Location - Frontline Centre, Lawrence Road

Starry Sunflower

Debs Haynes is one of a select band of lambie hunters who saw, stroked and snapped all 125 superlambananas. Well, stroked most of them... But she wasn't an early convert to the original SuperLambBanana. 'It grew on me I suppose,' she says. 'It used to annoy me that people kept drawing a bum on it!' But by the time *Go Superlambananas* arrived, she was hot on the trail.

'I'd done the cow parade in Manchester, but was a bit sceptical about whether Liverpool could do it. But we did it so much better. There was so much public buy-in. I got to be a tourist in my own city; I clocked nine miles round the city centre one day and know the city so much better. I went to see Tudorlambanana in Gateacre, and I'd never been there before. It's so close to the city, but so rural. Like Thornton Hough with a Scouse accent! I also made it to the top of Moel Famau and got a banana for being one of the first 500 up there. And I bumped into someone from work up there.'

So much did *Go Superlambananas* catch on at Unilever, where Debs works, that they bought a superlambanana to move around their Port Sunlight site. 'Quite a few of us at work got into it, and it all got quite competitive. But it definitely got us communicating. We have a pot of money which we can use for activities that enrich the lives of people at Unilever, and we used that for Billy, our lambie (named after Lever Brothers founder William Hesketh Lever),' she says. 'So we got in the artist Amanda Oliphant, who painted the Superlambananatree at Lime Street, and decorated Billy. He'll also be dressed up for occasions throughout the year – he had a witches' hat for Hallowe'en, and will also be celebrating Diwali, Christmas – and every other reason we can think of to dress him up!'

Artist - Alan Murray
Sponsor - Cosmopolitan Housing Group
Location - Olive Mount Gardens, Wavertree

238

LambMapBanana

'I'd seen Taro's work in Tokyo and he looked to be a very good sculptor. So I commissioned him to create something new — but we didn't know what he would come up with.

The rest is history.'

Lewis Biggs
Director
Liverpool Biennial

Artist - Claire Stringer
Sponsor - South Central Management Team,
Liverpool City Council
Location - Allerton Library

The Big Hope

Artist - Big Hope delegates
Sponsor - Liverpool Hope University
Location - The Gateway, Hope Park

Colours of Hope

*'Ja und die super
bananas waren herrlich und
Liverpool ist prima'*

Von Vera Smith und Ingrid Smith, taken from the Comments Book,
Go Superlambananas display, St George's Plateau, September 8 - 9

**Artist - Lauren Cheston and St Jerome's RC Primary School, Formby
Sponsor - Liverpool Hope University
Location - Taggart Lodge, Hope Park**

'Mandy' Mandala Superlambanana

Mandy Mandala links *Go Superlambananas* with 'Belonging – The Gathering', a Capital of Culture Four Corners commission, designed to engage local communities with cultural activity.

Her design takes inspiration from ancient mandalas, an eastern symbol of peace and oneness. During spring 2008, artist Patricia Lee ran workshops with local residents' associations to produce stained glass mandalas, which were used as tree decorations along Prince's Boulevard in Liverpool 8.

Now housed at Liverpool's World Museum, Mandy is made of more than 6,000 glass tiles. Her nose is made of millefiori (Italian for a thousand flowers) – sticks of rock made from glass, with a pattern running down the middle. The mandalas represent unity, hope and Liverpool's vibrancy and cultural diversity, challenging negative stereotyping of the area. She's also an example of one of the *Go Superlambananas* partnerships – a collaboration between Arts in Regeneration, the communities of Dingle, Granby and Toxteth, and Patricia Lee, funded by South Central Neighbourhood Management Team.

Mandy was sold for £25,000 at the *Go Superlambananas* Charity Auction in St George's Hall. David Fleming, director of National Museums Liverpool (NML), says: 'NML was determined to acquire at least one superlambanana for our collections… We didn't want to see them all disappear from public view. Imagine our dismay when the bidding for Mandy went beyond our reach, and our delight when Phil and Alexis Redmond ensured that Mandy was bought on our behalf. Now Mandy is owned by the people of Liverpool.'

**Artist - Patricia Lee, Arts in Regeneration
and the Communities of Granby, Toxteth and Dingle
Sponsor - South Central Management Team,
Liverpool City Council
Location - Princes Boulevard**

Superlamba-x-ray and child

*'Every child
should have one!'*

Taken from the Comments Book,
Go Superlambananas display, St George's Plateau, September 8 - 9

**Artist - Dominic Foster, Ashlea Haynes,
Liverpool Hope University fine art undergraduates
Sponsor - Liverpool Women's NHS Foundation Trust
Location - Liverpool Women's Hospital**

Cloudorama

Artist - Paul Cousins
Sponsor - Lady Lever Art Gallery, Port Sunlight
Location - Lady Lever Art Gallery, Port Sunlight

Past Port to the Future

*'A very banana
part of Liverpool's history,
have loved them and
will miss them.'*

Taken from the Comments Book,
Go Superlambananas display, St George's Plateau, September 8 - 9

**Artist - Clair Freeman
Sponsor - Port Sunlight Museum and Garden Village
Location - Port Sunlight Vision Museum, Wirral**

Superstegbanana

Artist - Designed by Mark Hendry, Team a go-go
Produced by Ben Cook
Sponsor - Ness Gardens, University of Liverpool
Location - Ness Gardens, Wirral

Lovemedoodle

'Prob the best bit of 08!!'

Cathy from Aigburth, taken from the Comments Book,
Go Superlambananas display, St George's Plateau, September 8 - 9

Artist - Designed by Adam Pitt
Produced by Alex Jackson
Sponsor - Virgin Trains
Location - London, Euston Station and Liverpool, Lime Street Station

The Highest Superlambanana

Generations of Liverpool kids and their parents have frolicked amidst the rural delights of Loggerheads in north Wales and climbed to the top of Moel Famau, cherished by Scousers as a 'very special piece of Liverpool'.

In 1926 the Crosville bus firm started a service from Liverpool to Loggerheads for day-trippers that triggered an affection for the locale that exists to this day. And during the Second World War many hundreds of children were evacuated to safety in the area.

In more recent times many thousands of youngsters – and older people – have enjoyed holidays at Liverpool City Council's Education Centre at Colomendy in Loggerheads, and will have undertaken the walk to the Jubilee Tower at the summit of Moel Famau.

It was very fitting, therefore, that the Moelfamaulambanana was 'put out to graze' in the summer of 2008 on the top of this well-loved mountain.

The Moelfamaulambanana was decorated by young people from numerous Denbighshire and Flintshire schools who created images relevant to that lovely and scenic part of Wales.

The sculpture was first seen at the International Musical Eisteddfod in Llangollen in July when it was on show during a series of workshops.

Artist - The Young People from Flintshire and Denbighshire Schools
Sponsor - Denbighshire County Council
Location - Moel Famau Country Park

SuperLambBanana

Ten years ago, a team of four – Andy Small, Julian Taylor, Tommy Reason and Ray Stokes – brought SuperLambBanana to life at Garston's Matchworks, basing the 17-foot beast on Taro Chiezo's miniature four-inch maquette.

The original SuperLambBanana was created using eight tonnes of concrete moulded around a frame of steel and wire mesh. It made an immediate impact. Julian says: 'I'd just finished college and my old tutor had been involved with creating the version that was in the Tate, which is around a third of the size of the finished one.

'We had Taro's maquette and made a mould so we could recreate it. While we were making it, we created a small hatch in its belly so we could climb in and out while we were adding the concrete exterior. When we completed the model, we thought it would be a great idea to seal the original plans inside as a sort of time capsule – we just didn't think there would be any requirement for them 10 years on. It's ironic that we've had to recreate it from scratch now, but there you go!

'It was a great project to work on, but not everyone liked it at first. Taro was really interested in Manga – this was pre-Pokémon, remember – and I think that's why kids always love it straight away. Sometimes adults aren't so sure.'

Taylor has seen SuperLambBanana's reputation grow and grow over the last 10 years. 'My brother saw a poster of it on the subway in Australia,' he says. 'He couldn't believe it. He literally said out loud: "That's the SuperLambBanana – my brother made that!"'

Taro Chiezo
Sculptor
Location - Avril Robarts Centre

Superlambswoolbanana

Artist - Ian Town
Sponsor - Wild in Art
Location - 08 Place, 36-38 Whitechapel

Both Sides of the Baaas

Artist - Paul Riley and students from NOCN Art Programme
Sponsor - HMP Liverpool
Location - HMP Liverpool, 68 Hornby Road, Walton

Tigerinthewoods

'I'm still painting superlambananas,' says artist Candida Boyes. 'They've taken over my life!' Candida's production line so far includes Rafa Baa-Nitez, Top Banana, Super St Domingo (the Everton lambie) plus a half-size version and four matching micro SLBs, Koppy, plus two half-size copies, Tiger in the Woods, Rover (the Tranmere Rovers team lambanana), the Duke (a desert camouflage recruitment SLB for Duke of Lancaster's Regiment), a Kenny Dalglish superlamb, which was the final surprise lot from the auction at St George's Hall – and a design by a pupil at Rainhill High School which is still in progress, including one full-size and two mini models. Phew.

The most prolific of the superlambanana contributors, Candida adds up her tally: 'I make that nine full-size, three medium and six mini, plus one for me – if I ever get time to paint him,' she laughs. 'Actually I sent in several designs in response to a call for designs, but none of them were chosen by sponsors,' she admits. 'Then I was asked to bring Rafa to life from a design created by the advertising agency Finch, which needed an artist to translate the 2D image into 3D superlambanana glory. They also designed Top Banana, Adidas-designed Koppy and I designed the rest. It's not fair to have a favourite – they've all been fun in different ways – but I'm proud to have painted all the football team SLBs (it's even made me take more notice of football!) – and Tiger was fun, as he was totally my own design... Top Banana was a challenge, tailoring his pinstripe suit in paint.'

Of the rest, she says: 'It's tricky to choose a favourite, but I'd probably say Cargo – it's thought provoking as well as intricate. But they've all got such colour and humour – I think that's why it's been a huge hit in Liverpool. It's accessible on so many levels and has involved so many people, either painting or just enjoying the creatures on the street.'

For the former designer-in-residence at Liverpool Playhouse and Head of Design for Mersey TV, it's been an unforgettable experience. 'Just the buzz of meeting and working with so many different artists from such diverse backgrounds has been great and the pleasure that so many people have had as a result. A very happy summer crowned with a huge sum for charity,' she says.

Artist - Candida Boyes
Sponsor - Sefton Borough Council and Liverpool Culture Company
Location - Roundabout on the Coastal Road and Shore Road, Ainsdale

Rover

Artist - Candida Boyes
Sponsor - Tranmere Rovers
Location - Prenton Park, Wirral

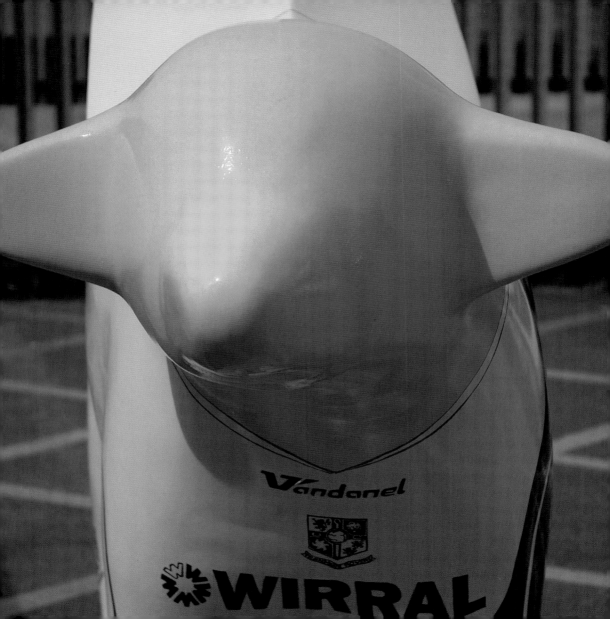

Springy

Artist - Pupils from Springwood Heath Primary School
Sponsor - Councillor Flo Clucas, John Clucas and Vera Best,
Allerton and Hunts Cross Ward
Location - School grounds on Danefield Road, L19

Happy Feet

'Bye bye my lambababas.'

Taken from the Comments Book,
Go Superlambananas display, St George's Plateau, September 8 - 9

Artist - Julie Edwards with pupils from Hunts Cross Primary School
Sponsor - Councillor Flo Clucas, John Clucas and Vera Best,
Allerton and Hunts Cross Ward
Location - Park close to Hunts Cross Library

278

2004 onwards

SuperLambBanana gets a makeover in 2004 as Liverpool looks forward to Capital of Culture year.

MARITIME

08
Liverpool
EUROPEAN

Lithuania meets Liverpool as city's handover of Capital of Culture

Go Super lambananas The Book

Mr Steve Rotheram shows Mayor of Vilnius Juozas Imbra...

...Liverpool yesterday ...Mayor of ...s, to the ...e handing ...tal of

...c heads, ...e Town Hall, ...tta ...their cities

...ozas Imbrasas,

who received a Superlambanana book and a Waterford crystal rosebowl, presented Cllr Rotheram with a white angel which is a symbol of Vilnius 2009.

Liverpool today passes its Capital of Culture title on to Vilnius and also to Linz, Austria, at a celebration event at the Pier Head.

Representatives from Linz, Stavanger – the non-EU Capital of Culture 2008 – and Liverpool's twinned city, Cologne, will arrive in Liverpool today to take part in the event.

Cllr Rotheram said: "Vilnius has a great year ahead and it was fascinating to meet Mr Imbrasas to find out more about their plans for 2009.

Go Superlambananas - a showcase of artistic endeavour and public participation in the city - becomes a book, is turned into Christmas tree decorations and gets publicity the world over...

way

ok **uperlambananas**
BARFORD/eb090109dculture-1

Bajoriniene said: "In we have already culture year party in the

ee ur of nt ning s term of so sees ew era y by

---

10 NEWS

Monday, December 22, 2008

Have yourself a little Lamby Christmas!

Have you got a lamby? Tell us all about it at liverpool echo.co.uk/forums

ECHO

LAMB LOVE: Three superlambananas bring a Liverpool touch of the Christmas story to a shop window in Bold Street

eb181208d

BY MICHAEL KETTIROS

LAMB-TASTIC: Lamby creator Taro Chiezo

LIVERPOOL shoppers are going Superlamb barmy

en years after the eight-ton original d in the city, and in the year 125 er lambies enhanced the streets apital of Culture, miniature lambies are flying off the shelves as soon as they arrive.

With only three shopping days until Christmas, time is running out for people to bag themselves one of the most sought after festive presents on Merseyside.

Utility, in Bold Street, took delivery of more than 80 of the porcelain figures statues

a long waiting list for the sought-after

as to when their next shipment will arrive.

Irene Ryan, who works at the Heritage Centre shop in St George's Hall, said: "A delivery is expected any day now.

"We don't know how many lambananas we'll receive. But whatever we do get sell out within days."

The 08 Place in Whitechapel received 60 miniatures last Saturday.

But they had also vanished from the shelves by mid-week in the continuing Superlamb bonanza.

The city centre tourist information centre has sold more than 500 of the miniatures in the past three months.

The plain yellow design has proved to

Christmas creations.

Retailers say the demand for all things lambanana also extends to key rings, calendars, colouring books and postcards.

A glossy hard-back book featuring all of the 125 uniquely-decorated lambies which entertained people over the summer has also proved a hot yuletide buy.

Nearly every copy of Go Superlambananas: The Book, was sold within a fortnight of being launched by Merseyside publishers **Cities500**.

Photographer Guy Woodland, of Cities500, said: "We've sold the run of 6,000 books in two weeks - it must be some kind of record."

284

Advertising agency Finch worked with Wild in Art to create a map of the superlambanana trail. 'We wanted people to behave like tourists in their own city,' said Sally-Ann Wilkinson. 'We planned to take them to the tourist spots, but also to cover as many as possible of Merseyside's five boroughs.' Merseytravel printed the maps and more than 200,000 were snapped up as the people of Liverpool hit the streets.

ALBERT DOCK

BATH STREET
KING EDWARD
OLD HALL STREET
OLD LEEDS ST.
PALL MALL
GREAT CROSSHA
119
HATTON GARDEN
17 ST. PAUL'S SQ.
18
15
16 VIRGINIA ST.
20
19
PRUSSIA ST.
22 23
EMUND ST.
BIXTETH ST.
24
OSMOND ST.
GEORGE ST.
26
TITHEBARN STREET
VERNON ST.
MOORFIELDS
DALE STREET
CROSSHALL ST.
PRINCES PARADE
13
NEW QUAY
25
27
CHAPEL STREET
29 30
EXCHANGE ST.
14
28
31
41
12
32
WATER STREET
VICTORIA STREET
40 39
ST. NICHOLAS
21
STANLEY ST.
ST. NICHOLAS PLACE
11
33
NORTH JOHN ST
35
MATHEW ST.
43
Royal Liver Building
THE STRAND
CASTLE ST.
COOK ST.
WHITECHAPEL
44
Water Street
CANADA BOULEVARD
9
10
34
CHURCH
Cunard Building
BRUNSWICK STREET
37
61
Port of Liverpool Building
JAMES ST.
LORD ST.
PARADISE STREET
Bluecoat
MANN ISLAND
NORTH JOHN ST.
COLLEGE
36
STRAND STREET
CANNING PLACE
HA
8
CANNING
WAPPING
LIVER ST.
PARK LANE
6 7
5
3
1 2
4
WAPPING

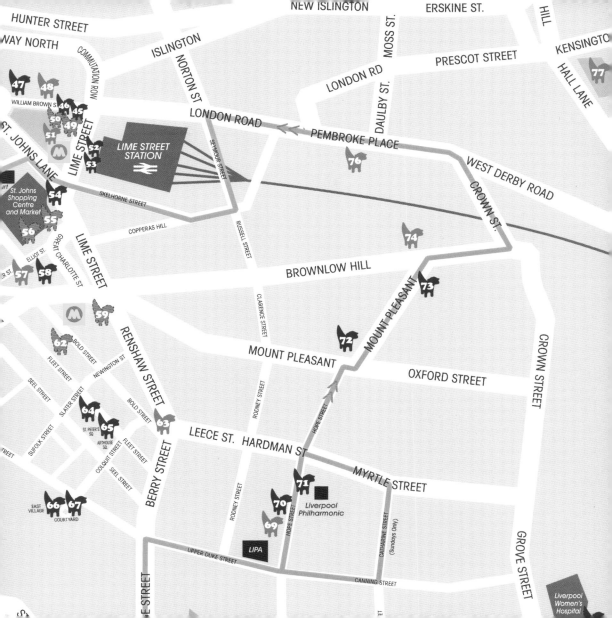

Index

Index

Creating the trail...

The stats behind *Go Superlambananas*

100 litres of varnish

1 iconic sculpture

half a million raised for charity

8 tonnes of concrete

100 cans of spray paint

400 litres of paint

26 community groups

125 superlambananas

30,000 mosaic tiles

£42 million generated in economic benefit for the city